THIS ANNUAL BELONGS TO:

MARKRUSSON

THE BEGINNING

BY TIM HAINES, SERIES PRODUCER, WALKING WITH DINOSAURS

A long time ago, I hatched the idea of doing a Natural History programme about dinosaurs.

Walking with Dinosaurs was a project that took four years to grow and mature into a complete picture of what it was like to live in the lost world of these giant reptiles. This awesome annual shows you that world. The gentle giants and swift killers that dominated earth for 160 million years. And, of course, the tonnes of fun and hard work that went into bringing dinosaurs to life on the screen.

Enjoy it for yourselves – we did!

TRESPASSERS WILL BE EATEN!

WALKING WITH DINOSAURS

CONTENTS

AN

NUAL 2001

DITOR   **Sarah Armstrong-Prior**
ART EDITOR   **Nikki Davies**
PRODUCTION EDITOR   **Steve Smith**
ILLUSTRATIONS   **Dave Jukes**
WRITTEN BY   **Sarah Armstrong-Prior,**
                              Rob Bright, Dr Paul Chambers
SCIENTIFIC ADVICE   **Professor Mike Benton,**
                              Dr Paul Chambers
INTRODUCTION   **Tim Haines, Series Producer,**
AND SERIES ADVICE   **Walking with Dinosaurs**
COMMISSIONING EDITOR **Jaynie Senior**

PICTURES   **BBC commissioned photographs**
                              © BBC Worldwide 1999, except...
Cover by Radio Times/Framestore;
following pictures © Yorkshire Museum:
Tuojiangosaurus (p4), Dr Manning & fossil (p11)
Dr Manning and T rex model (p31).

Thanks to Phillip Manning and the Yorkshire Museum.

These animals lived 'millions of years ago'. We got tired writing that so from now on you'll see 'mya' instead!

BACK TO LIFE... BACK TO REALITY!

It took nature over 3,300 million years of evolution to produce the dinosaurs. The last living dinosaur vanished from the earth over 65 million years ago. Walking with Dinosaurs had just three years to try to bring the dinosaurs back to life for television. This was to be a tall task.

Since dinosaurs were first discovered there have been many attempts to figure out what they would have looked like and how they would have behaved. The first attempts were a complete disaster. Walking with Dinosaurs had to do better...

Obviously, no human has ever seen a living and breathing dinosaur, but we do have their fossils and these can give us a lot of information.

Scientists can take the bones of the dinosaurs and put them together to form a complete skeleton. By looking at a dinosaur skeleton we can roughly tell what shape and

Fossil skeletons, such as this Tuojiangosaurus at the Yorkshire Museum, help scientists understand more about dinosaur anatomy.

A very strange-looking Ornithocherius on location in New Zealand.

Can you tell what it is yet?

size it would have been when it was alive.

Further clues, like the fossilised spines or plates that run along the backs of dinosaurs like Stegosaurus, or the large bony clubs on the tails of the likes of Polacanthus, have also been found.

Walking with Dinosaurs took all of this information and made very accurate models of those dinosaurs needed for the series. These are some of the most accurate models of dinosaurs that have ever been made... even paper models like the one to the left here!

It's very fierce... honest!

The next step was to find somewhere for the dinosaurs to live...

THERE'S NO PLACE LIKE HOME...

To bring the dinosaurs to life, Walking with Dinosaurs had to find those places on Earth which the dinosaurs would be able to call home...

There are very few parts of the modern world which the dinosaurs would recognise, let alone be able to live in!

Since the death of the dinosaurs, Earth has undergone many changes. The climate, plants, landscape and coastlines are now all very different to what they were like in the Mesozoic era. Could Walking with Dinosaurs really find areas on the modern planet that the dinosaurs could call home?

Scientists looked at the fossil plants and animals that have been found in the same rocks as dinosaur bones. They then used these fossils to understand which trees and creatures would have lived with the dinosaurs.

During the dinosaurs' lifetimes, they saw quite a few changes – after all, dinosaurs lived for over 160 million years. The environments in which they lived changed several times, even the continents didn't manage to sit still!

Similarly, different dinosaurs preferred to live in different places, just like modern animals.

Walking with Dinosaurs took what we know about each of these animal's habitats and scoured the Earth for suitable places for their dinosaurs to live.

Their search was successful and film crews were dispatched to remote places in New Zealand, Chile, New Caledonia, California and the Bahamas. A home from home had been found for the dinosaurs at last!

Tasmania

New Zealand

Redwood forest, California

New Caledonia

Plantlife proved one of the most important factors in choosing the filming locations. Certain plants had to be flown in (left) or even made up, like this one below!

5

DINO Myths

THE FIRST DINOSAUR FOSSIL WAS FOUND OVER 180 YEARS AGO. SINCE THEN THERE HAVE BEEN MANY MISTAKES MADE ABOUT DINOSAURS. BE SURE YOU'RE NOT CAUGHT OUT BY THESE COMMON DINOSAUR MYTHS AND LEGENDS!

IF IT'S BIG, GREEN AND SCALY, IT'S A DINOSAUR!

When the first giant reptile fossils were found it was not always clear which ones were dinosaurs and which ones belonged to other reptile groups. All dinosaurs are reptiles but not all large reptiles are dinosaurs! True dinosaurs lived on land and had legs that were directly underneath their body.

TOROSAURUS

THESE WERE DINOSAURS TOO!

Postosuchus – Looks like a dinosaur but its legs are on the sides of its body.
Ornithocheirus – No! Dinosaurs don't fly!
Liopleurodon – Although some dinosaurs could probably swim short distances they could not live in the water.
Birds – Evolved from small meat-eating dinosaurs and are their closest relatives but are NOT true dinosaurs.

DINOSAURS AND HUMANS LIVED TOGETHER!

No! By the time the first humans appeared on the Earth the dinosaurs had been gone for almost 65 million years! This means that there is no way that Fred Flintstone could have had a pet dino!

T REX

ALL DINOSAURS WERE HUGE AND VICIOUS!

Dinosaurs came in all shapes and sizes. Some, like Diplodocus, were bigger than a house, but Leaellynasaura was not much bigger than a turkey! They also ate many different types of food. Large dinosaurs like T rex and Allosaurus would have been terrifying meat-eaters but most of the biggest dinos, like Brachiosaurus and Diplodocus, only ate plants.

ALL DINOSAURS LIVED ON EARTH AT THE SAME TIME!

Films like *Jurassic Park* like to put different dinosaurs together at the same time. But, just as humans and dinosaurs did not live at the same time, neither did many types of dinosaurs. For example, by the time of T rex and Torosaurus, dinosaurs like Stegosaurus and Allosaurus had been extinct for well over 90 million years.

DINOSAURS WERE SLOW AND STUPID!

Some older books and films like to show the dinosaurs as being slow and clumsy with very little intelligence – this is wrong.

Like all animals, dinosaur bodies were well adapted to surviving within their chosen environment. The very big dinosaurs would have moved slowly because of their size. But some of the smaller meat-eaters like Coelophysis could run very fast indeed, perhaps to escape from other dinosaurs. Some say that T rex, which weighed over five tonnes, could have run twice as fast as an Olympic athlete!

Some plant-eating dinosaurs such as Stegosaurus did have very small brains but then they did not need to do much thinking! However, meat-eating dinosaurs would need to have had more intelligence in order to outwit their prey. Troodon, a ferocious dinosaur from the Cretaceous, is thought to have been one of the brainiest dinosaurs.

DINOSAURS RULED THE EARTH!

Perhaps because they were so big and so many, we sometimes think that dinosaurs must have ruled the Earth during the 160 million years they were alive.

While they were undoubtedly the most obvious land animals of their day, they shared their world with many other creatures such as insects, mammals, birds, amphibians and other types of reptile during the Mesozoic era. No one group of animals really ruled the Earth, as they were all dependent on each other for their survival.

DINOSAURS ARE STILL ALIVE!

In 1912 the famous author Sir Arthur Conan Doyle wrote a story called *The Lost World* in which scientists found some dinosaurs living in the Amazon jungle.

Similarly, some people believe that there may still be dinosaurs living in very remote parts of the world such as the Congo Basin in Africa. Despite many expeditions in search of these dinosaurs, nobody has yet come back with proof that dinosaurs are still alive.

POSTOSUCHUS

THE Mythical QUIZ

HAVING EXPOSED A FEW DINOSAUR MYTHS, CAN YOU DECIDE WHICH OF THE FOLLOWING ARE TRUE OR FALSE?

1. A T rex could have eaten a Stegosaurus for lunch!
2. Today there are dinosaurs living in the Amazon jungle!
3. The dinosaurs lived on Earth for over 160 million years.
4. The birds and dinosaurs are closely related to each other.
5. A Stegosaurus would have been brainier than a Troodon.
6. A Tyrannosaurus rex could run faster than a human.
7. An Ophthalmosaurus was a dinosaur.
8. The biggest dinosaurs got that way because they ate so much meat.

ANSWERS:

1: False – they lived at different times.
2: False – there is no solid evidence that dinosaurs are alive today.
3: True.
4: True – the birds evolved from the dinosaurs.
5: False – it's the other way round.
6: True – T rex is thought to have been a nippy mover.
7: False – it was a marine reptile.
8: False – the biggest dinosaurs were nearly all vegetarian.

DINO D[

WHO DISCOVERED THE DINOS AND WHERE AND WHEN DID THEY FIND THEM? CHECK OUT OUR WORLD MAP WHICH SHOWS SOME OF THE MOST SIGNIFICANT DINOSAUR DISCOVERIES TO DATE!

MORRISON FORMATION

WHEN: 1877

DINOSAUR DETECTIVES:
Arthur Lakes found the first fossils. The same year two palaeontologists, Othniel Marsh and Edward Cope, started work at the formation.

DINOSAURS DETECTED:
Diplodocus, Brachiosaurus, **Allosaurus** (above), Stegosaurus, Ornitholestes.

OTHER STUFF!
Many fossils of crocodiles, lizards, fish and mammals have also been found here.

HELL CREEK

WHEN: 1906

DINOSAUR DETECTIVE:
Henry Fairfield Osborn

DINOSAURS DETECTED:
Tyrannosaurus rex, **Ankylosaurus** (below), Anatotitan, Torosaurus.

PETRIFIED FOREST

WHEN: 1920s

DINOSAUR DETECTIVE:
Charles Camp, a palaeontologist from the University of California.

REPTILES DETECTED:
Postosuchus, **Placerias** (below), metoposaurs and cynodont teeth.

DINOSAUR DETECTED: Coelophysis.

OTHER STUFF!
Many fossil plants including horsetails, cycads, ferns and araucaria.

GHOST RANCH

WHEN: 1947

DINOSAUR DETECTIVE:
The site was discovered by Edwin Colbert.

DINOSAURS DETECTED:
Coelophysis (right).

OTHER STUFF!
Other fossils include fish, phytosaurs, clams and crayfish.

PATAGONIAN DESERT

WHEN: 2000

DINOSAUR DETECTIVE:
Dr Philip Currie and a team of palaeontologists from Argentina and North America.

DINOSAUR DETECTED:
Unnamed as yet, but may be as many as six creatures preserved at this site.

DINO DATA EXTRA!
The dinosaur is thought to be related to the Giganotosaurus and possibly the largest meat-eating dinosaur discovered so far at just under 14m long.

?

SCOVERIES

OXFORD CLAY

WHEN: 1860-1915

DINOSAUR DETECTIVE:
Alfred Leeds, an amateur fossil collector who was based near Peterborough.

REPTILES DETECTED:
Mainly fish and marine reptiles found at this site. The icthyosaurs: Ophthalmosaurus, **Cryptoclidus** *(above left)* and Liopleurodon.

WEALDEN FORMATION

WHEN: 1825, 1841, 1983

DINOSAUR DETECTIVES:
Gideon Mantell, Richard Owen, William Walker.

DINOSAURS DETECTED:
Iguanadon *(right)*, Hylaeosaurus (similar to Polacanthus), Megalosaurus, Baryonyx.

SANTANA FORMATION

WHEN: 1971

DINOSAUR DETECTIVE:
Llewellyn Price discovered the first dinosaur fossils.

REPTILES DETECTED:
Pterosaurs such as Ornithocheirus and **Tapejara** *(above right)*.

OTHER STUFF!
Other fossils include fish and invertebrates.

DINOSAUR COVE

WHEN: 1989

DINOSAUR DETECTIVE:
Miners and palaeontologists alike were involved at Dinosaur Cove.

DINOSAURS DETECTED:
Leaellynasaura holotype *(right)*, Atlascopcosaurus (related to Iguanadon and Anatotitan) and Timimus (from same group as Coelophysis).

DIGGING FOR DINOSAURS!

OVER 1,000 SPECIES OF DINOSAUR HAVE BEEN DISCOVERED SO FAR, AND WE'RE STILL DIGGING! SO WHAT DO THE DINO DETECTIVES LOOK FOR?

FOSSILS

Fossils are the remains of plants and animals which existed millions of years ago. They are made when an animal dies and becomes buried in the soil before it rots away... or gets eaten! Over the years and with a bit of natural chemistry thrown in the bodies turn into stone, ready to be discovered by anyone who knows how and where to look.

DIY DINO DIG

SO, ARE YOU READY TO DIG THAT DINO? HERE'S HOW!

FIND YOUR SITE

There are two ways to do this, the hard way and the easy way! The hard way is to dig your own, for example in your garden. The easy way is to find a place that has already been 'dug' by nature. Good places are cliffs, beaches, valleys, canyons, hillsides and quarries. Remember, wherever you choose you must get permission first and it is always better to have an adult with you on your dig.

GRAB SOME GEAR

You will need a small paintbrush, hammer and chisel. You might also need something to protect your find, like plastic sheeting or bubble wrap as well as a collecting bag. Fossils can be very delicate as they are so old so if you do find something be careful! You don't want to discover a new species then destroy it three seconds later!

Could you 'dig' being a professional fossil hunter?

YOU WOULD NEED:

Patience of a saint!
Each speck of rock must be individually removed so that the precious bones are not damaged. This could take weeks, months – or years.

Sun cream and deodorant!
Baking hot deserts are often the site of fossil 'digs'.

Spare underwear!
This life can mean working in wild, remote and dangerous parts of the world such as terrifying canyons that could flood at any minute.

SEARCH FOR THOSE SKELETONS!
Look for stones with unusual shapes or patterns. The edges might be either very jagged or very smooth, depending on what you're looking for. Think about it: bones and teeth come in pretty set shapes, if not standard sizes!

EXCAVATION TIME
Gently break up any hard or compact rock around your potential fossil using the hammer and chisel – but watch out for your fingers. Then, use the paintbrush to carefully brush away the rock and earth around it until your fossil is free. If you can clear enough space around the fossil, slide your plastic sheet underneath your find before you lift it out of the ground so that if it starts to break up, at least you'll have all the pieces!

AND FINALLY...
Clear up your mess and report any finds to your local museum or find out where your nearest dinosaur club is – there are plenty around! Check out our dino address book on page 60 for a few pointers.

FAMOUS DINO DETECTIVES

● **Mary Anning** (1799-1847) was a British fossil hunter. She found her first fossils before she was even a teenager. Among her discoveries were the first fossilised plesiosaur and icthyosaur to be found.

● **William Buckland** (1784-1856) was a British fossil hunter as well as a clergyman and Oxford don. He discovered Megalosaurus in 1819 and named it in 1824. It was the first dino ever described scientifically and the first dinosaur carnivore (theropod) discovered.

● **Edward Cope** (1840-1897) was an American palaeontologist who named just under 1,000 species of fossil animals. Among the dinosaurs he named was Coelophysis in 1889.

● **Earl Douglass** (1862-1931) was another US fossil hunter who, in 1909, found what we now call Dinosaur National Monument in Utah, USA. He found around 350 tonnes of fossils, including Allosaurus, Apatosaurus, Diplodocus and Stegosaurus.

● **Sir Richard Owen** (1804-1892) was a British man who coined the term Dinosauria (dinosaur), recognising them as a group of large extinct reptiles. He proposed this new name in an article published in 1842. Owen also built the first dinosaur park in 1854 at Crystal Palace, London. It still stands today, and shows some rather odd-looking dinosaurs which don't look as we know them today.

DINOSAUR

GREAT, GREAT, GREAT GRANDPA
STEGOSAURUS
AGED 160 MYA

● **STEGOSAURUS**

Length: 13m.
Height: 7m.
Weight: 7 tonnes.
Group: Stegosaurs.
Lived: Late Jurassic, 160-145 mya.
Eating habits: Herbivore.
Walked: On four legs – quadruped.
Distinctive features: A row of massive bony plates down its back and a dangerous tail with four spikes to tackle predators.
Fascinating facts: The first fossil was found in Colorado, USA in 1877.

FAMILY ALBUM

STEG'S NEPHEWS, THE TWINS BRAD AND BRETT

BRACHIOSAURUS

AGED 160 MYA

SWOT POINTS!

Brachiosaurus = 'arm lizard'.
This may seem odd as he didn't have 'arms' like you'd imagine.
His name actually refers to the fact that, unlike other dinosaurs, his front legs were longer than his hind ones, so that his back sloped upwards towards the head. Also, at 80 tonnes, Brachiosaurus was 20 times heavier than a large elephant!

● **BRACHIOSAURUS**
Length: 23m.
Height: 13m.
Weight: 70-80 tonnes.
Group: Sauropods.
Lived: Late Jurassic, 160-145 mya.
Eating habits: Herbivore.
Walked: On four legs – quadruped.
Distinctive features: It's got to be that long neck!
Fascinating facts: Brachiosaurus could graze from tree tops that no other sauropod could reach.

DRAW A TOROSAURUS!

THINK YOU COULD CUT IT BEING A DINOSAUR ARTIST? WE'VE MADE IT EASIER BY DRAWING HALF ON A GRID, JUST LIKE THE ONES SOME REAL ARTISTS USE!

TOROSAURUS FACTS

This sociable, three-horned herbivore roamed the earth about 67-65 mya, and could weigh about seven tonnes.

3 STEPS TO A TERRIFIC TOROSAURUS!

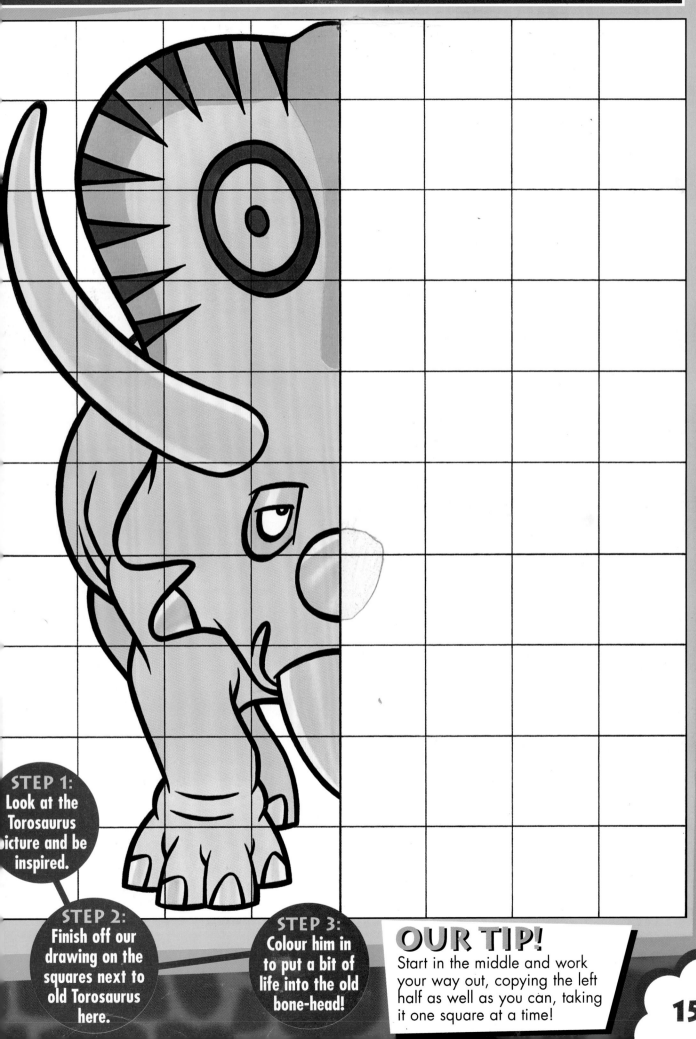

STEP 1:
Look at the Torosaurus picture and be inspired.

STEP 2:
Finish off our drawing on the squares next to old Torosaurus here.

STEP 3:
Colour him in to put a bit of life into the old bone-head!

OUR TIP!
Start in the middle and work your way out, copying the left half as well as you can, taking it one square at a time!

THE BIG INT

The great thing about palaeontology is that we're only just beginning to scratch the surface. People are just now beginning to do more digging in Africa, South America and China. And completely new dinosaurs are turning up.

THE PROJECT

What was the idea behind the series?
We wanted to do something about palaeontology but we also wanted to make it something very popular and interesting to put on BBC1 – so that was the starting point. And then we thought, well, if you are going to want to watch re-creations they'd better be good because everyone has seen *Jurassic Park*. Every week people go to the cinemas and see great graphics so television had to catch up.

Was it difficult bringing the dinosaurs back to life so realistically?
No, the principles and the technology were laid out in *Jurassic Park*. What you see there is a real background, lots of actors running about screaming and then a computer graphics creature put in afterwards. I was very fortunate to bump into a man called Mike Milne from Framestore who had worked with this kind of

The team (clockwise from left): Mike Milne (Framestore director), Jez Harris (dinosaur designer), Jasper James & Tim Haines (producers).

technology for a long time. And although in principle I knew what I wanted, technically I had no idea how to go about it – that was what he did.

Who picked the filming locations?
I employed someone to go round and look at likely sites. Basically she had a big fat ticket to travel around the world and take pictures of it all! Really, there wasn't a great deal of choice because we had to avoid grass but find all sorts of rare plants. So it was

> "ALTHOUGH IN PRINCIPLE I KNEW WHAT I WANTED, TECHNICALLY, I HAD NO IDEA HOW TO GO ABOUT IT."

never that difficult to choose between locations, as we were just desperately trying to find the right place to do any filming at all!

So you didn't go then?
No, I went to see Chile and California because she couldn't get there, but otherwise it wasn't until the filming that I saw the places for myself.

Can you tell us about something you have learned through working on Walking with Dinosaurs?
I'm much more interested in plants now than I used to be. I used to be what you might call 'green-blind', not normally bothering to look into the background of a scene. But now I go round saying, 'Look at those wonderful araucaria!' And whoever I'm with will say, 'Hummm, it looks like scrappy old pine to me!' There are some fantastically rare and wonderful species around.

Were you involved in any other dino projects or ones about other animals before this one?
No, no dinosaur programmes. I was in the Natural History Unit where I was a radio producer for a while and then working in TV on a programme called *Nature*, which was more of an environmental show really.

When you started the project, did you realise how long it would take? Three years seems a long time!
Yes, I mean, big landmark documentaries can take two or three years, usually just one to two years, but this one I knew would be longer.

How much involvement did you have when it came to the animation side?
Jasper James was the producer of two of the programmes – I made four of them. Our job was simply to be the approval person at every single stage, so we would talk to all the scientists and stuff like that. I chose everyone we were going to work with right from the beginning, then Mike chose his animation team and his specialists. I then got the 'macquettes' (models) made, the 'sculpts' made and I approved them, I approved all the animatronics for my programmes – Jasper, the other producer did his – then I'd cut it.

Did you draw any original sketches to help them along?
No, that's where you can go to the scientists if you need something because they're perfectly capable of producing sketches and things.

What was the most difficult thing you had to do on Walking with Dinosaurs and why?
Actually, probably the most difficult thing was sitting around all day long when clouds kept going in front of the sun. It isn't until you get somewhere and rely on that consistent sun that

you realise how clouds can come and mess up what you are trying to do. You have to sit there waiting for exactly the same light level – you can't go for hazy light, because then all the lighting references would be wrong, for example. That can become a real mind-numbingly tedious thing to do if you have got a lot of stupid clouds around!

> "EVERYONE HAS SEEN JURASSIC PARK... SO TELEVISION HAD TO CATCH UP."

Was there any particular shot that was the most difficult?
Well, we had problems with a camera mount on a helicopter for the shot where we fly over the trees and see a column of Iguanodon walking along the beach. The camera mount was fixed down wrongly which meant it had a bit of a judder. In post-production they had to get rid of this judder. And that was an immensely complicated shot anyway,

because you had to have all these Iguanodon, making sure they do a few different things so it doesn't look too repetitive. The camera is on the helicopter anyway, there are little dots on the beach marking everything out – so it was an absolute nightmare. That one shot took a year to make in the end. It was very, very difficult.

TIM AND DINOSAURS

What would be your advice to people who want to get into this sort of thing?
I'd say you should just become interested in animals and biology really, because dinosaurs were animals! One thing I'd point out is that to understand them don't think of them as monsters, just think of them as ordinary animals going about their business like a blackbird might do in your garden.

Those trouble-making Iguanadon! But don't they look brilliant?

What do your family think, do they like dinosaurs?
Well, the three-year-old is too young to appreciate them – it's just, 'Roar!' dinosaurs, and running about. The eldest likes them and she's just started a new school where she is very popular because her daddy did Walking with Dinosaurs!

Which is your favourite dinosaur and why?
Um, I'm always asked that one and I have never had a very good answer – in fact, I think I've said a different one each time! But I tend to say that he's not a dinosaur, but I love Liopleurodon, because he was so huge and so hungry! I remember when we did the pilot I measured him out on the beach because we would later have him beached at the end of programme three. And I remember being stood there looking from tail to head and thinking, 'That's ridiculous! No animal can be that big!' But he's a truely impressive carnivore. He's the one I'm most frightened of – or would be if I met him!

Which dinosaur do you think is the most resourceful?
One of the traits of all the dinosaurs is that they are very adaptable, very flexible and successful because of that. Coelophysis was an animal who wasn't the biggest, wasn't the nastiest, might not even have been the fastest but, for some reason, he and his kind would take over. And despite all the other giant hungry reptiles that lived there – he'd be terribly successful.

TIM NOW...

You have just won an award. Can you tell us what that was and what it was for?
Best documentary of 1999 with the Television and Radio Industry Council, called TRICK. Cilla Black received a lifetime achievement award at the same time – we shared a moment! It was quite funny actually because it was a very light entertainment, showbizzy thing, but they have to have a documentary category in there and we trogged up, no one knowing who on earth we were. I said, "Sorry, our stars couldn't turn up but they didn't like the menu!"

Are there any more dinosaur projects coming up?
We've got one coming out for Christmas – it's called

The Ballad of Big Al. I don't know if that will be the final title. It is based on a wonderful skeleton in Wyoming which was dug up in 1991. It's an almost complete teenage Allosaurus, who had a really rough life – he's covered in wounds and bumps and injuries. We know a lot about the Allosaurus, they're a very common dinosaur found in North America from the late Jurassic, so what we are going to do is to re-tell the story of his life and how he came to an untimely end just before adulthood, with obviously one or two wounds along the way.

Any more after that?
Well, we're doing a series after that, but I can't say what it is at the moment. There are lots more fantastic extinct creatures to come. We want to go on showing people new creatures they have never seen before.

SPEAK & SPELL

HOW ON EARTH DO YOU PRONOUNCE THOSE LONG NAMES?!

AL-oh-SAW-rus	ALLOSAURUS
ah-NAT-oh-TIE-tan	ANATOTITAN
ang-KYE-luh-SAW-rus	ANKYLOSAURUS
BRACK-key-uh-SAW-rus	BRACHIOSAURUS
SEE-luh-FIE-sis	COELOPHYSIS
CRIP-tuh-CLEE-dus	CRYPTOCLIDUS
SIGH-no-dont	CYNODONT
die-NON-E-kus	DEINONYCHUS
di-PLOD-doh-KUS	DIPLODOCUS
you-STREP-toh-spon-DIL-us	EUSTREPTOSPONDYLUS
i-GWAN-uh-don	IGUANODON
lay-EL-ee-nuh-SAW-ra	LEAELLYNASAURA
LIE-oh-PLOO-row-don	LIOPLEURODON
MUT-uh-BUR-uh-SAW-rus	MUTTABURRASAURUS
op-THAL-mo-SAW-rus	OPHTHALMOSAURUS
OR-nith-oh-KYE-rus	ORNITHOCHEIRUS
PLAH-sare-EE-as	PLACERIAS
PLAH-tee-oh-SAW-rus	PLATEOSAURUS
POH-luh-KAN-thus	POLACANTHUS
POST-o-SOOK-us	POSTOSUCHUS
RAM-for-RINK-us	RHAMPHORHYNCHUS
STEG-oh-SAW-rus	STEGOSAURUS
TAP-ah-JAR-uh	TAPEJARA
TOR-oh-SAW-rus	TOROSAURUS
tie-RAN-oh-SAW-rus RECKS	TYRANNOSAURUS REX
YOU-ta-RAP-tor	UTAHRAPTOR

WHAT'S IN A NAME?

- **Dinosaur** (dino + saur) = 'terrible lizard'
- **Dino** comes from deinos = 'terrible'
- **Saurus** comes from the Greek = 'lizard'

The term was first used by the British scientist **Sir Richard Owen** (1804-1892) to describe some fossil remains which did not look even vaguely like any living creatures.

WHAT A NAME!

Here are two of the funnier and weirder ones...

ANATOTITAN = giant duck! Latin **anas** = duck + Greek **titan** = giant

DIPLODOCUS = double-folded bearing beam (eh?!) Greek **diplax** = double-folded + Greek **dokos** = bearing-beam

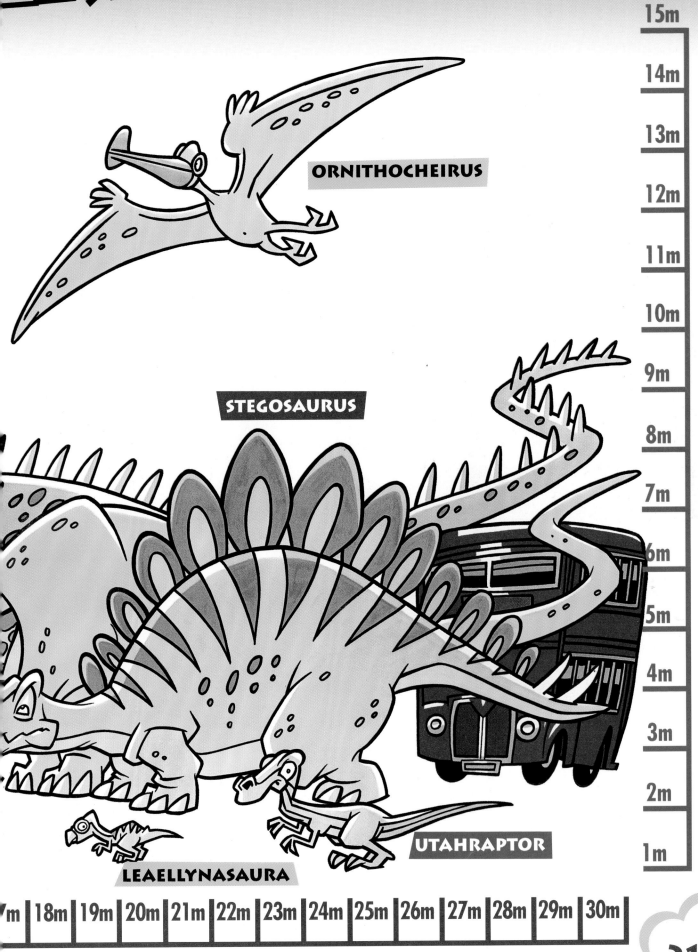

ORNITHOCHEIRUS

STEGOSAURUS

UTAHRAPTOR

LEAELLYNASAURA

15m
14m
13m
12m
11m
10m
9m
8m
7m
6m
5m
4m
3m
2m
1m

m | 18m | 19m | 20m | 21m | 22m | 23m | 24m | 25m | 26m | 27m | 28m | 29m | 30m

CAUGHT ON CAMERA!

SO, YOU'VE GOT YOUR LOCATIONS, YOU KNOW WHAT YOU WANT, NOW ALL YOU'VE GOT TO DO IS FILM THE INVISIBLE ACTORS!

This was the task faced by the crew working on Walking with Dinosaurs.

The technology used to make the series was based around a type of filming called 'photo-real' where you try to 'composite' or put artificial characters into a real background and make it look like it's all real. Sounds tricky? Well, it is. Because, although the technology is great, it can only be as good as the material it's given to work with. That's where the cast and crew of Walking with Dinosaurs came in....

No, this dinosaur isn't drinking! The team are pouring some syrupy liquid into the model's mouth to look like saliva.

Dinosaur designer Jez Harris helps out with Ornithocheirus' make-up!

One of our divers shows some puzzled Australian children a model of Ophthalmosaurus.

Reference shots needed to be taken for each bit of the finished programme that had a dinosaur or reptile in view.

SOME OF THE CREW WERE BECOMING JEALOUS OF THE ATTENTION THE DINOSAURS WERE GETTING...

Forget the dinosaurs, guys. Let's do some jousting instead!

I want to play with the dummy, let me do it!

Look, I can do the 'Tapejara', it goes something like this!

Yes! I love this bit!

Ah, BLOOD, lovely BLOOD!

FACT CHECK

REMEMBER...

● Walking with Dinosaurs was shot in seven locations: New Zealand, Australia, Tasmania, Chile, California, the Bahamas and New Caledonia.

● It took a total of 27 full weeks of filming over a period of 14 months.

● The film crew averaged ten people. The typical film crew for a natural history/documentary programme is around a hundred!

● Framestore and BBC teams worked and played together to produce the end result of six programmes, a pilot and a behind-the-scenes documentary.

WE COULDN'T HAVE DONE IT WITHOUT YOU!

DINOSAUR

GREAT, GREAT GANGSTER CLAN
COELOPHYSIS ("ICE-C")
AGED 220 MYA

● **COELOPHYSIS**

Length: 2-3m.
Height: Just under 1m at hip.
Weight: 35-40kg.
Group: Early theropods.
Lived: Triassic, 222-215 mya.
Eating habits: Carnivore; occasional cannibal!
Walked: On two legs – biped.
Distinctive features:
Aggressive pack-hunter. This lot got a bit snappy when they were hungry and would often fight over their food!

FAMILY ALBUM

COUSIN YUSEF
EUSTREPTOSPONDYLUS
AGED 162 MYA

● **EUSTREPTOSPONDYLUS**
Length: Around 5m.
Height: Over 2m when rearing!
Weight: 500kg.
Group: Theropods (Ceratopsian).
Lived: Late Jurassic, 165-160 mya.
Eating habits: Carnivore, scavenger.
Walked: On two legs – biped.
Fascinating facts: Only one fossil found so far, which was from a quarry north of Oxford, UK.

One thing about Yusef
– he was always hungry!

JURASSICA!

CAN YOU WALK WITH THE DINOSAURS AND SURVIVE? STEP INTO THEIR WORLD AND PLAY THE SCARIEST GAME OF YOUR LIFE!

ENTER

RULES

FIGHT OR FLIGHT
Roll the dice and fight your nearest predator. Whoever rolls the highest number gets to run on... this time.

TRIASSIC FLY-BY
SHORT CUT: You're in luck! Race 4 spaces ahead by taking the short cut to number 8.

SAFETY IN (ODD) NUMBERS
Roll a dice. If you get 2, go back 2, roll 4, go back 4, get a 6 and go back 6. Roll an odd number and stay put till your next go!

EXTINCT
You would never have survived with the dinos about. Start again, and be more careful!

PADDLE POWER
SHORT CUT: Smart move! A baby Cryptoclidus has offered you a ride, you take it to number 15!

DICE WITH DEATH
Miss a go or play **Fight or Flight** with your nearest dinosaur enemy!

1

FIGHT OR FLIGHT
2

3

TRIASSIC FLY-BY
4

5

SAFETY IN ODD NUMBERS
6

7

8

9
EXTINCT: Tapejara got hungry!

26

ESCAPE

EXTINCT:
Volcano erupts as
you walk by
(typical!)

20

19

18

17

16

FIGHT OR FLIGHT

15

10

14

PADDLE 11 POWER

12

DICE WITH 13 DEATH

DINO DY

SO WHEN WERE ALL THESE GIANT DINOSAURS STOMPING ABOUT THE PLANET? A LONG, LONG TIME AGO! TO GET AN IDEA OF JUST HOW FAR BACK WE'RE TALKING, IMAGINE HISTORY FROM THE DINOSAURS TO HUMANS SPREAD OUT OVER A DAY.

Midnight – 220 mya

The Triassic period. The first dinosaurs live on a huge single continent called Pangaea.
Climate: There was no snow at the poles so it was warmish all over the world. There were massive storms and hot dry deserts across the equator.
Reptiles: Placerias,

Allosaurus

Stegosaurus

Climate: In the early Jurassic the Earth was mostly dry, but it became wetter and wetter.
Dinosaurs: Diplodocus, Brachiosaurus, Allosaurus, Stegosaurus, Ornitholestes. Also Anurognathus – a pterosaur.

Postosuchus   **Placerias**

Peteinosaurus

Postosuchus, Cynodont, Peteinosaurus.
Dinosaurs: Coelophysis, Plateosaurus.

11am – 127 mya

The early Cretaceous period. Some of the modern continents are starting to take shape with the north of Pangaea known as Laurasia and the south called Gondwana.
Climate: The land was often flooded by

Iguanodon

8am – 155 mya

The late Jurassic period. Pangaea is starting to break up although South America, Africa and Australia are all still one land mass.

rising sea levels, so it kept getting wetter. The first flowers also appeared.
Dinosaurs: Iguanodon, Polacanthus, Utahraptor.
Reptiles: Ornithocheirus and Tapejara – pterosaurs.
Birds: Iberomesornis.

Diplodocus

NASTY

Tyrannosaurus rex

2pm – 106 mya

The mid-Cretaceous period and a big land mass has moved to the South Pole. The continents are drifting away from each other.

Climate: Sea levels reached their highest in this period. On the land it was warm with plants and flowers everywhere.

Dinosaurs: Leaellynasaura, Dwarf Allosaur, Muttaburrasaurus. Also Koolasuchus – a large amphibian.

Leaellynasaura

7pm – 65 mya

Earth looks pretty much as it does today and the dinosaur era is almost over. India floats towards Asia for a collision that will start to form the Himalayan Mountains.

Polacanthus

Ornithocheirus

Tapejara

Climate: The Earth began to get colder and life at the North and South Poles started to die out, although they weren't yet frozen over.

Dinosaurs: Tyrannosaurus rex, Torosaurus, Ankylosaurus, Anatotitan.

11.58pm – 200,000 years ago

Earth as we know it! Modern humans have arrived and are starting to make a mess. There are no dinosaurs left but their relations are still around. There is a huge range of animals and plants living on the planet.

Climate: The Earth's surface has a varied and ever-changing climate, colder closer to the poles and warmer towards the equator.

Reptiles: Of the reptiles from which dinosaurs evolved, turtles, crocodiles, lizards and snakes remain.

Birds: Birds are almost living dinosaurs, having evolved from small meat-eating dinosaurs.

Mammals: The warm-blooded, hairy mammals were around in the age of the dinosaurs, but they rule the Earth today.

LIFESPAN

The larger dinosaurs had longer lifespans than smaller ones. The age development of a Diplodocus was like that of humans in some ways. They didn't reach full maturity until they were over 20 years old. Some of the oldest females may have been 100 years old. Tyrannosaurus rex could also live to about this age, while the sea giant Liopleurodon could rule the oceans for over 150 years!

WORKING WITH DINOSAURS

DINOSAURS MAY BE FUN TO READ ABOUT OR SEE IN MUSEUMS, BUT WHAT IF YOU WANT TO SPEND YOUR DAYS WORKING WITH DINOSAURS? HERE'S OUR GUIDE!

▶▶▶▶▶▶▶▶▶▶▶

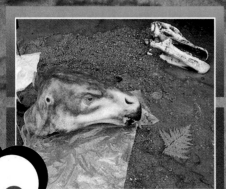

BE A PROFESSIONAL FOSSIL-HUNTER

About 130 years ago, there was a great rush in North America to find dinosaur bones. Why? To get specimens for research, to be able to name new species, to amaze people and museums, and also, to get rich!

This was when some of the best-known dinosaurs – such as Diplodocus, Stegosaurus and Tyrannosaurus rex – were discovered. Many of the specimens in natural history museums around the world were discovered and sold at this time.

Between 1900 and 1970, the dino-digging frenzy seemed to die down. More recently, the hunt has begun again, with some 10-15 new species being found every year.

Nowadays, there are probably over 100 professional dinosaur scientists around the world excavating dinosaurs, but for research – not for sale.

BE A PALAEONTOLOGIST

The scientists who work with fossilised remains of dinosaurs are called palaeontologists and use many different techniques to try to understand how dinosaurs lived.

They take bones and teeth to reconstruct the shape of their bodies to see how they must have moved and what they would have eaten when alive. They look at plant and animal fossils that have been found with the dinosaurs to work out what type of landscape they would have walked on.

Modern palaeontologists must use the latest machinery and computers to look inside dinosaur bones and to understand their chemistry. All this needs lots of training.

BE A DINOSAUR ARTIST

Dinosaurs are now so popular that people do not just want to see their bones in museums, they also want to know how they would have looked and behaved when they were alive.

Although palaeontologists can work out how dinosaurs would have lived and breathed, it is up to dinosaur artists and sculptors to bring them back to life in books, displays and films.

These artists are very talented people. Not only must they be good sculptors or illustrators, but they also have to be able to look at a dinosaur skeleton and understand where its muscles and skin would have gone. They also have to imagine what each dinosaur was like and then give its skin a realistic texture and colour.

When they are finished, the artists' drawings and sculptures are often used in books about dinosaurs or in museum exhibits. Sometimes the work of these artists is animated for films or even for TV programmes, just like Walking with Dinosaurs!

BE A DINOSAUR SPECIALIST IN A MUSEUM

We caught up with Dr Phillip Manning, and asked him to tell us all about his job. Here's what he said…

"My rather old-fashioned title is 'Keeper of Geology'. It's a bit of a throwback to the 19th century when the post was first invented! My job entails carrying out research into new types of beasties from our ancient past! For example, I'm currently working on a new species of dinosaur from the Yorkshire coast. My job also includes cataloguing these many thousands of specimens and making exhibitions about the collections we have… but mainly about dinosaurs!

I also dig dinosaur bones and track dinosaur footprints throughout the UK – this is the fun part of the job! Currently I'm working on two excavations, one of a Jurassic-aged ichthyosaur from Whitby and the other removing some middle Jurassic-aged dinosaur tracks from a 'secret' location on the Yorkshire coast.

My main area of specialism with dinosaurs is how the limbs function. I also focus on how and why dinosaur tracks look the way they do.

One favourite part of my job, which I almost forgot, is what I have been doing over the last two days and will also be doing on Sunday – public talks and demonstrations about dinosaurs, fossils, etc. I give these to audiences of children of all ages! The talks and demonstrations are probably the most rewarding part of my work.

Most people are fascinated by dinosaurs and it's great being able to make the facts even more amazing than the myths.

As I always say, may your tracks be long and your thoughts deep!"

Dr Phillip Manning, Keeper of Geology, Yorkshire Museum.

GOT SOME QUESTIONS ABOUT DINOSAURS? WELL, WE'VE GOT THE ANSWERS TO SOME OF THE MOST FREQUENTLY ASKED QUESTIONS ABOUT DINOSAURS. CHECK THEM OUT...

DINO YOU KNOW?

How many dinosaurs were there altogether?

We can't say for sure. Scientists know of over one thousand dinosaur species, but new ones are being discovered all the time. In fact, at least twenty new species were named in 1999 alone.

Did dinosaurs lay eggs like crocodiles do?

Yes, just like modern reptiles, dinosaur mothers laid eggs in nests on the ground. Even though

A newly-hatched Diplodocus.

some dinosaurs were huge, their eggs seem to have been really quite small. Even the largest one found is only about five times bigger than a chicken's egg.

Which dinosaur was the fiercest?

Although the tyrannosaurs may have looked the fiercest, the dromaeosaurs such as Utahraptor, were probably the fiercest overall, in terms of cunning, determination and range of weapons.

Can we tell which dinosaur was the strongest?

The strongest would probably have been the one with the biggest muscles, but as muscles don't become fossilised, we presume it would be the largest and heaviest one. Some scientists say the largest known dinosaur is probably Seismosaurus from New Mexico, USA. However, in 1994 new bones were dug up belonging to a huge dinosaur. US palaeontologists now think it may be the biggest so far. They have called it Sauroposeidon, and think it stood 18m tall and weighed around 60 tonnes – 30 times bigger than a giraffe!

What was the smallest dinosaur ever found?

We can't say for sure, as we're still finding new dinosaur fossils, but one of the smallest known dinosaurs so far is Compsognathus. Skeletons of two of these dinosaurs (which appear to be of adults) show a length of 0.7 to 1m long, and may well have been the tiniest.

Is it possible to bring back the dinosaurs?

Only on TV and in Hollywood, that's why

How long ago did dinosaurs live?

Dinosaurs lived millions of years ago. The first ones appeared around 230 million years ago and the last ones died out over 65 million years ago. If you do your sums, that means dinosaurs walked the earth for 165 million years – which is 75 times longer than humans have walked at all!

Were there dinosaurs in the sea?
Only if they fell in! Like most other reptiles, dinosaurs lived on land and had dry, scaly skins. There were no true

sea-dwelling dinosaurs, but some may well have been able to swim. However there were reptiles that lived in the sea at around the same time as dinosaurs existed. One example is Cryptoclidus, shown here.

programmes like Walking with Dinosaurs are so cool! Lots of people think you can make a new dinosaur from old DNA, but that's very unlikely, and impossible today at any rate. Bad luck!

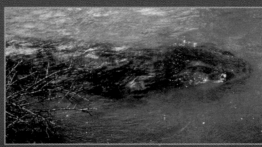

How did they decide which mammals and amphibians, like Koolasuchus, to include in Walking with Dinosaurs?
(We didn't know the answer to this one, so we asked Tim Haines to explain…)
"Each programme was based on a very big fossil site from where we gathered as much information as possible. Because the programmes show different times in dinosaur history we wanted to spread them out and cover major points in dinosaur evolution. We quickly came

down to half a dozen sites that were appropriate. We used Koolasuchus *(left)*, for instance, because we wanted to do something in the Poles and the best Polar finds were down in Australia and just represented this weird ecosystem in which Koolasuchus happened to also live. The whole point of doing programme five was actually that you are used to seeing dinosaurs in big herds or on big plains, and we wanted to show them somewhere different – in a little forest, where it was dark for half a year, just to show that dinosaurs did live all across the world in totally different places."

ANAGRAMOSAURUS

Unscramble the letters to see which dinosaur is revealed. The pictures will give you a clue!

1 TATINA... NIA

2 ZAIDA NOUGN

3 SLUR ALA SUOS

4 DCSLIPRY TFCOUU

5 TCUPH SOSSUO

6 RETOSS AGSU USU

PIECE BY PIECE

We've mixed up three ancient reptiles – can you work out which ones they are?

TIMEWARP WORDSEARCH

```
S A U R O P O D Y I S P Z V B U C F F Y L L S C W
G C W X W L J Z P B U G L S F T Z U G Z A D G Z Z
E O R E Z C C K W P O J T P V J S G X J M F C N K
S H N E V M P C O N W S N D J S M U K N W U E B R
V K O D T I A A P D M P P V G J E N C H Q L Y V E
T E E L W A D D L R R G A E B B P A Z P R I C B P
D R X L U A C E D A I E B L C U C A L H K Z W G T
C I I T E E N E N G E C P T E I D A N T O A T Y I
X H N A I T V A O C O O A L V O M X A G V R F G L
S I G O S N O O L U E D N B I S Z E H N A D Y J E
L Q L P S S C N L A S O B T F C S O N B U E Y V N
L V T S C A I T O U N X N P O C A U I X J L A V L
N A I G A O U C E V T D I L S L T W N C H C G Y C
E B D K J C N R H M G I V P S K O X B Y P P O V J
O C E A N U A T C Z S N O A I X H G A G F F E W D
W F V Z B U A M I O M E W N L J B Z Y W U H D I M
A I O J N W J C B N V B F M E S O Z O I C E R A P
W P N T N K I V V R E E I O L W B Y R Z H F R E E
Q Q I J H S R J T N I N H P U Q G U A J F W Z A J
I E A D S O V W E X B A T I E Z Y N O L V N O R O
K B N A N I Z G Y P F C N B Q D R Y M N A T A T M
H X R Z F M R F B G T L W U Z Z T O K N A A F H A
H U P D Z A I U P M V W J P V J Y S P L J W T J C
J O R J O R Y X A W W Z B Z Z J J Y S D F S A N V
V X V E C E H W S T L S N L Y D B J H W H R V S M
```

CAN YOU FIND THE HIDDEN WORDS?

Mesozoic Era
Cretaceous
Specimen
Extinct
Biped
Pangaea
Gondwanaland
Dinosaur Cove
Lizard
Contintent
Palaeontology

Triassic
Cambrian
Skeleton
Ocean
Replica
Devonian
Evidence
Fossil
Jurassic
Reptile

Earth
Sauropod
Evolution

THESE DINOSAURS DIDN'T ALL LIVE DURING THE SAME PERIOD – BUT WHAT IF THEY HAD? WHO WOULD HAVE BEEN THE MOST FEARSOME REPTILE OF ALL TIME?

DINOWA

THE CONTENDERS...

Prepare yourself for an earth-shaking contest as we match up the toughest of the giant lizards to find out who really was the king of the dinosaurs. Here's a look at the prize fighters...

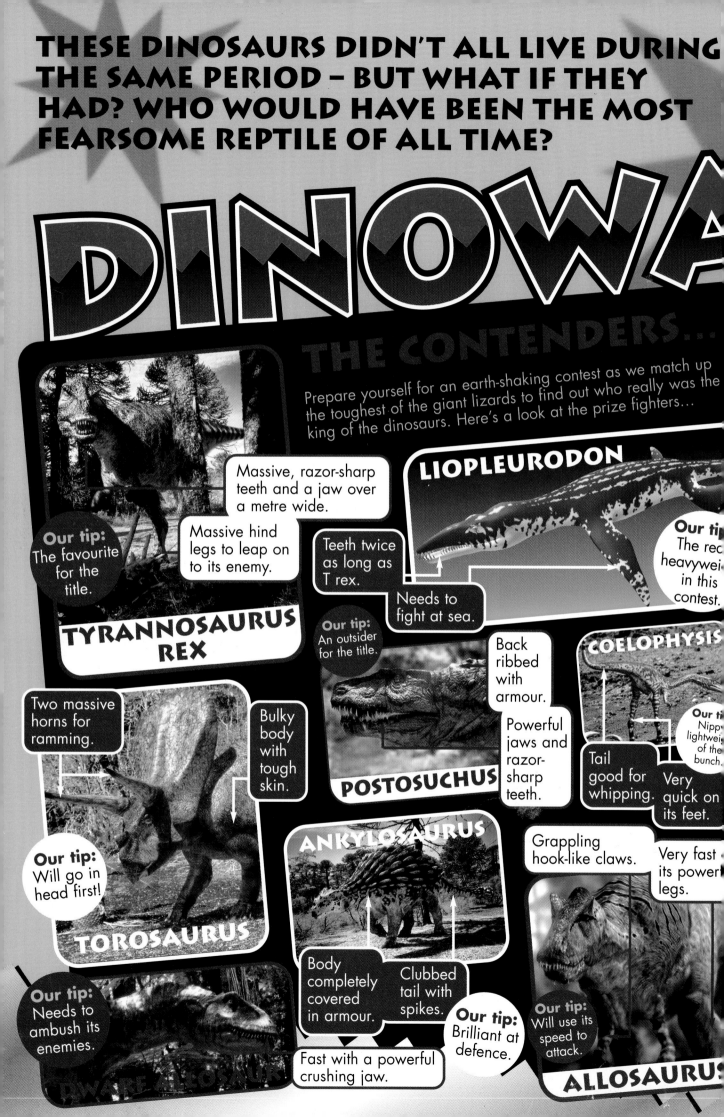

Massive, razor-sharp teeth and a jaw over a metre wide.

Massive hind legs to leap on to its enemy.

Our tip: The favourite for the title.

TYRANNOSAURUS REX

LIOPLEURODON

Teeth twice as long as T rex.

Needs to fight at sea.

Our tip: An outsider for the title.

Our tip The red heavywei in this contest.

Two massive horns for ramming.

Bulky body with tough skin.

Back ribbed with armour.

Powerful jaws and razor-sharp teeth.

POSTOSUCHUS

COELOPHYSIS

Our tip Nippy lightwei of the bunch.

Tail good for whipping.

Very quick on its feet.

Our tip: Will go in head first!

TOROSAURUS

ANKYLOSAURUS

Grappling hook-like claws.

Very fast its power legs.

Our tip: Needs to ambush its enemies.

Body completely covered in armour.

Clubbed tail with spikes.

Our tip: Brilliant at defence.

Our tip: Will use its speed to attack.

Fast with a powerful crushing jaw.

DWARF ALLOSAUR

ALLOSAURU

RS!

THE MATCH!

T rex v Postosuchus
Two legs take on four in this battle between one of the earliest dinosaurs and one of the latest. While Postosuchus defends bravely thanks to its armour, T rex uses its massive jaws.

WINNER: Tyrannosaurus rex

Allosaurus v Coelophysis
Coelophysis uses its speed to avoid the lunging jaws of the Allosaur but this is a fight it can't win. When Allosaurus finally captures its opponent in its mouth, it's over in an instant.

WINNER: Allosaurus

Ankylosaurus v Torosaurus
A close contest this one. Torosaurus stabs with its horns but Ankylosaurus has awesome protection in its armoured body. After Torosaurus has exhausted itself, a hammer tail by Anklyosaurus causes a fatal blow to the body.

WINNER: Ankylosaurus

Liopleurodon v Dwarf Allosaur
Dwarf Allosaur waits by the beach for its opponent. But the contest is over before it even has a chance to fight. Liopleurodon has come crashing out of the water, grabbed it in its mighty jaws and disappeared again.

WINNER: Liopleurodon

THE SEMI-FINALS

WE'RE DOWN TO THE FOUR TOUGHEST DINOSAURS AROUND...

Liopleurodon v Ankylosaurus
Ankylosaurus walks fearfully along the water's edge. Liopleurodon emerges and opens its jaws. Ankylosaurus swings its hammer tail and beats it off. But Liopleurodon attacks again and this time drags Ankylosaurus to a watery grave.

WINNER: Liopleurodon

T rex v Allosaurus
This is a tough contest. Allosaurus uses its speed to tease Tyrannosaurus but T rex makes the most of its size. Its massive jaws grab Allosaurus by the neck and soon the fight is over.

WINNER: Tyrannosaurus rex

DINOWARS!

THE FINAL

Tyrannosaurus rex v Liopleurodon

The fiercest land dinosaur takes on the king of the sea. The battle is long as Liopleurodon lunges out to snap at Tyrannosaurus. T rex fights back with its razor sharp teeth but Liopleurodon's teeth are even bigger and it takes an enormous bite at T rex. The giant land lizard stumbles about and then collapses. Liopleurodon drags its defeated opponent into the sea.

WINNER: Liopleurodon

THE CHAMPION

Although few of these dinosaurs would ever really meet, there's no doubt that at 25m long with a jaw up to 5m in length, no land dinosaur would be a match for the Liopleurodon. The king of the sea is also the king of the dinowars!

DINOWORLD

WHAT WAS GOING ON IN THE DINOSAUR NEIGHBOURHOODS? WHICH OTHER CRITTERS AND BEASTIES WERE AROUND? TAKE A LOOK AT THESE...

WATER BABIES

Coelacanth
This medium-sized carnivorous fish survives today but was most common during the Triassic.

Liopleurodon
This massive sea-dwelling reptile lived during the Jurassic, 165 to 150 mya. At 25m long, Liopleurodon had four flippers, each more than 3m long. This huge sea creature had a massive 5m skull and very sharp teeth! At that size, it's no surprise that Liopleurodon was the largest and most powerful carnivore ever to have lived.

Cryptoclidus
This marine predator usually hunted alone for his meals of fish and squid. Cryptoclidus (main picture) appeared in the late Jurassic, living between 165 and 150 mya. At 8m long, Cryptoclidus had a 2m long neck with a 60cm skull and could weigh up to 8 tonnes.

Ophthalmosaurus
These Jurassic swimmers (below) looked like modern dolphins. They were 5m long with a 1m skull and also fed on fish and squid. They had big eyes, which probably meant they could hunt at night.

Ammonite
This spiral shell is a sea creature related to today's octopus and squid.

Hybodus shark
A dangerous Jurassic predator for young icthyosaurs like Ophthalmosaurus.

Koolasuchus
This beast (below) was a large amphibian that haunted the shores during the early

Cretaceous, 140 to 112 mya. At over 5m long, he had a massive skull with powerful jaws. As a carnivore, this came in handy! He would even have been able to tackle small dinosaurs to add to his normal diet of fish and crustaceans like crab and lobster.

Deinosuchus
Crocodiles were common by the Cretaceous period. So far, the largest found is Deinosuchus (meaning 'terrible crocodile'). He may have been 15m long and weighed about 2 tonnes!

Also around at this time were belemnites, some crabs, turtles, lungfish, frogs, crayfish, crinoids and algae, to name just a few!

DINOWORLD

AIR

Peteinosaurus

Peteinosaurus *(right)* was a flying reptile which appeared in the Triassic period, living between 228 and 215 mya. This little flier ate insects – his favourite food were dragonflies, which tended to be quite a bit bigger than they are today. He had short wings that stretched only 60cm long, with a long, stiff tail and a skull of 6cm. That's this big!

←——————— 6cms ———————→

Rhamphorhynchus

Rhamphorhynchus *(above right)* was a late Jurassic flier, living between 170 and 145 mya. He had a wingspan of up to 2m and was 1m long, including his tail – not quite so big as Ornithocheirus would be! These carnivorous fliers were social pterosaurs, probably because of safety in numbers, and gathered in noisy flocks on relatively

LAND

Cynodont

Cynodont is actually a name for a broad group of mammal-like reptiles, which include the direct ancestors of modern mammals. Cynodontia *(shown above)* lived in the late Triassic, between 222 to 215 mya. They were omnivores, eating anything from small reptiles to bugs, eggs and roots. The Cynodont was up to 1.5m long and weighed up to 20kg.

● Postosuchus

Postosuchus *(below right)* was a really mean carnivore which evolved in the late Triassic! He was up to 6m long, able to rear up to 2m tall and weighed just under a tonne. He had a short but broad skull with deep powerful jaws. His armour included a row of plates covering his long back. Postosuchus was an archosaur, on the line to crocodiles but not a crocodile himself.

● Placerias

This sturdy mammal-like reptile *(far right)* was around in the late Triassic, living between 222 and 215 mya. Placerias was a herbivore and used his tusks to search the soil for roots and tubers. He would also have eaten clubmoss and low-level ferns. Placerias was up to 3.5m long and a tonne in weight, and would have been safer from dinosaurs if he roamed in groups. His cheek horns would have also come in handy for defence.

● Steropodon

Steropodon was an early mammal. At 50cm long, he looked like a giant hedgehog! He lived during the early Cretaceous and was mainly a

safe, predator-free islands where they could feast on fish in peace.

Ornithocheirus

Ornithocheirus *(top right)* ruled the airwaves long before radio, during the Cretaceous, 125 to 110 mya. His wingspan was 12m and he could glide over great distances. With just one flap of his giant wings he could travel several kilometres across ancient skies. He weighed over 100kg and fed on fish.

Tapejara

This marine pterosaur *(left)* lived during the early Cretaceous, between about 120 and 110 mya. His most distinctive feature was his brightly-hued

head crest which was up to 1m tall. With a wingspan of up to 5m and a body 1m long, a 25kg Tapejara would have made for a striking sight!

Iberomesornis

This Cretaceous flier *(above right)* was a small bird that lived around 115 mya. Iberomesornis was an omnivore, feeding on anything it could get its claws and beak into, possibly including freshwater shellfish.

Also around during the dinosaur days: butterflies, dragonflies, moths, lacewings, sphecid wasps, damsel flies and a whole range of other insects.

scavenger, feeding on grubs, insects, dinosaur eggs and dead animal carcasses. His modern-day descendant is the Australian spiny echidna.

● Didelphodon

Didelphodon *(above)* was an early marsupial which lived during the late Cretaceous, between 67 to 65 mya. This pouched mammal is related to the modern opossums found 'down under'! He was an omnivorous scavenger, feeding on small reptiles, insects and animal carcasses, as well as any dino eggs he was able to steal. Didelphodon was about the size of a badger at 1m long. He was one of the largest mammals of his time and weighed about 20kg.

Animals: Scorpions, phytosaurs, Dinilysia (early snake), Tuatara.

Plants: Cycads, araucaria and ferns, maiden hair, clubmoss and, later, some flowering plants like magnolia.

DINOWORLD DATES:

What Happened When…

- **230 mya** – The first mammals emerge.
- **200 mya** – Frogs and salamanders start to evolve from the earlier amphibians.
- **170 mya** – Crabs and lobsters appear.
- **130 mya** – Plants such as magnolia arrive.
- **67-65 mya** – The early marsupial Didelphodon appears. Its relatives today include the opossums, which are found in Australia and New Zealand.

FOSSIL

FOOL YOUR FRIENDS WITH THESE FALSE FOSSIL FINDS – FIND OUT HOW TO FAKE IT HERE!

FOSSIL KIT

- Large margarine tub
- Air drying clay
- Household sponge
- Plaster of Paris
- An old bowl
- Paints: brown, grey (or black & white)
- Water in a cup
- Paintbrush
- Palette knife or ruler
- An adult to help you buy (!) and mix the plaster of Paris.

DIY TIME!

1 Place some clay inside a margarine tub and flatten it with your fingers, making sure it is deep enough (about 3-4cm deep) to make the ammonite shape.

2 Make the shape by creating a spiral pattern in the clay with your finger. Start very small and work your way out, then make some lines inside the ammonite shape using a palette knife or the end of a ruler. You can smooth the clay, by dipping your finger in water and lightly brushing the clay.

Photography by Christopher Baines. Made by Natalie Abadzis. Thanks to Abigail.

FURY!

3 Mix up some plaster of Paris with water in an old bowl, until the plaster is thick and creamy, then empty this on top of your clay fossil shape and leave to set. This will take a few hours, but always read the instructions on the plaster of Paris.

This is what it will look like before you pour on the plaster of Paris...

4 When the plaster cast has set, take it out from the tub, being very careful not to crack the plaster cast. You may need to cut the margarine tub from around the cast.

5 Paint the fossil using an old sponge. Dip a household sponge into some paint and build up layers of colour by sponging on white, black and brown paint. This will help give the fossil an old-looking effect.

You can use this technique to make any sort of fossil you want. We reckon some dinosaur teeth and bones would look pretty cool!

HERE ARE SOME WE MADE EARLIER!

ART(Y) FACTS AND TIPS!

● You can use nearly anything to make marks and textures in clay – twig, finger, ruler, palette knife, etc.

● Remember, fossils are pretty ancient, so the more battered and rough-looking you make it, the better – so be as messy as you want!

● Help get rid of some of the air bubbles in the plaster of Paris by flicking the underside of the margarine tub while the plaster is setting.

● Always follow the instructions on the plaster of Paris. You can buy this and clay from good craft shops and mail order catalogues.

● And finally... here's Phil Manning (left) from the Yorkshire Museum with the real thing!

LEA'S LIFE

A YEAR IN THE LIFE OF A LEAELLYNASAURA

Muttaburrasaurus stomping around in search of large plants to eat. Meanwhile the Dwarf Allosaurs hide among the thick tree trunks waiting to pounce on unsuspecting prey, like my family. In the icy cold waters, an odd-looking creature called Koolasuchus lurks about trying to catch fish in its enormous 80cm jaws. But our most fearsome enemy is not a dinosaur but the winter itself, which leaves our continent in freezing darkness for four whole months.

A Muttaburrasaurus.

Koolasuchus waits for lunch!

THE TIME: 106 MYA...

THIS IS ME!

My name is Lea Leaellynasaura, although my friends call me Princess! I'm quite short for a dinosaur – my dad is the tallest of us and he's only just over 2m long and 1.3m high. My most attractive features are my huge, wide eyes, which allow me to see really well. This comes in handy, especially during our long dark Polar winters. Apart from that, I'm a vegetarian and consider myself quite sociable for a dino! I live in a clan with some fellow Leaellynasaura, and I'm proud to say that my mum and dad are the leaders. Apparently they're the 'dominant male and female' – whatever!

LEA'S HOME

About 106 mya, the South Pole was a large continent covered in dense forests, containing land that would later split away and become South America and Australia. As well as my family, the trees tremble with the movement of

SPRING

The sun is out at last! We've been struggling to find food for the last four months in complete darkness! Already the males are fighting with each other, although they rarely end up kicking or biting. If one of them was injured it would be bad for the clan!

We're all busy building and protecting our nests at the moment. Some of our biggest enemies, the long-haired Steropodon bullies, have turned up to try and steal some of the eggs. I used my

Our family look for food in the forest.

little arms to shove dirt in their faces. It was enough to make them run off this time, but I know they'll be back.
I can hear the sound of our look-out making clicking noises. That means the coast is clear. Not looking forward to the summer though. That dreaded Allosaur will be arriving from the north.

I wonder if I'll have a brother or sister?

SUMMER

Summertime, and the sun will be up in the sky for the next five months. The eggs have hatched and the hatchlings are making pests of themselves. We have to keep a constant eye on them to make sure they don't wander off. If they do, they're done for. They're quick learners though, and are already practising their sprints and jumps. Handy for escaping Allosaurs.

The whole clan takes time out to get some sleep. We can't sleep for long though, in case we get spotted by a meat-eater. Fortunately our camouflaged skins keep us pretty well-hidden among

It's a brother AND a sister!

Keeping a look-out for the Allosaur.

these trees and ferns. If one of those Allosaurs does see us, at least the look-out will warn us.

AUTUMN

The sun is starting to get lower but the weather is still fine. We came up against a rival clan today. They were trying to invade our patch in the forest. If we wanted to make sure we had enough food we couldn't let that happen. Everyone stood together and shouted as angrily as we could at them. It was enough to scare them off.

Huge herds of Muttaburrasaurus have headed down our way from the north. We decided to follow them because they always leave loads of half-eaten plants on the forest floor. Had to be careful though. They've got

massive feet and I could easily have been crushed.

WINTER

Bad news today. With winter coming the Muttaburrasaurus have been leaving the forest and the racket they made meant we couldn't hear a warning call from one of the clan. He was warning about an Allosaur ambush, but for one young male it was too late. He was caught and eaten. The whole clan is very frightened.
The sun has finally set but we're still busy. Our big eyes mean we can hunt for things like fungi among the rotting

Too late – a sad end for one of the clan.

bark. When it gets really cold, we all gather in a huddle to keep warm and go into semi-hibernation for a couple of days. Our mission now is to survive the winter. Can't wait for spring to come around again!

Brrr! Winter's here again.

We have to watch out for the Muttaburrasaurus' big feet!

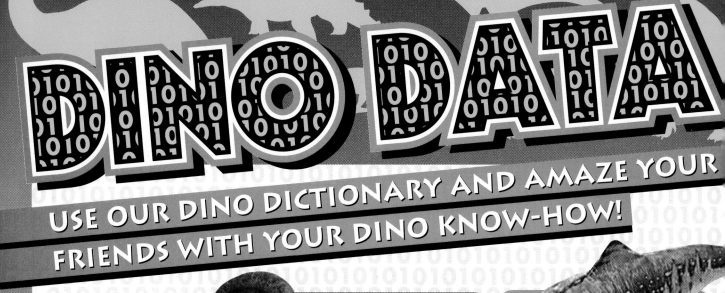

DINO DATA

USE OUR DINO DICTIONARY AND AMAZE YOUR FRIENDS WITH YOUR DINO KNOW-HOW!

AMPHIBIANS
The first air-breathing animals with backbones. They can live both in and out of water. Modern amphibians include frogs and salamanders.

ARCHOSAURS
A group of reptiles which gave rise to dinosaurs, pterosaurs and even crocodiles. The word archosaur literally means 'ruling reptiles'.

BIPED
Creature which usually stands or walks on two legs. (Bipedal = two-footed).

CRETACEOUS
This period of the Mesozoic era lasting between 144-65 mya.

CARNIVORE
An animal that eats other animals as its main food source.

DINOSAUR
Literally means 'terrible lizard'. A group of land-living reptiles that are now extinct.

EVOLUTION
The process whereby animals and plants change and develop over millions of years.

FOSSIL
Buried plant and animal remains from millions of years ago that have turned as hard as stone and been preserved in rock. Scientists have learned a lot about ancient life from fossils.

GONDWANALAND
The southern part of the huge land mass called Pangaea which stretched from pole to pole millions of years ago.

HADROSAURS

Also called duck-billed dinosaurs, these were a group of bird-hipped reptiles, like this Anatotitan *(left)*. They had long powerful hind legs and smaller front ones. They also often had elaborate bony head crests.

HERBIVORE
An animal that feeds only on plants, and is specially adapted to do so.

ICTHYOSAURS
These were sea-dwelling dolphin-like carnivorous reptiles, such as Ophthalmosaurus *(above)*.

JURASSIC PERIOD
The name of the period which lasted between about 205 mya and 144 mya during the Mesozoic.

KOOLASUCHUS
A carnivorous amphibian *(right)* who lived in Australia during the early Cretaceous period.

LAURASIA
The northern part of the land mass called Pangaea.

LIZARD-HIPPED
(See Saurischian)

MESOZOIC ERA
The name given to the time between about 250-65 mya. The major periods in this era were Triassic, Jurassic and Cretaceous.

ORNITHISCHIAN
These dinosaurs were one of the two main types of dinosaurs. They were bird-hipped, with both lower hip bones pointing down and backwards.

PALAEONTOLOGIST
A scientist who studies fossils to learn about ancient life.

PLESIOSAURS
The name given to a group of marine reptiles which included marine crocodiles and icthyosaurs *(right)*.

PROSAUROPODS
A group of early, lizard-hipped dinosaurs that included Plateosaurus *(right)*. They appeared during the Triassic and died out during the Jurassic period.

PTEROSAUR
Literally means 'flying reptile', such as these Tropeognathus *(below)*. They were not dinosaurs, but lived at around the same time.

QUADRUPED
A creature that usually stands or walks on four legs.

REPTILE
One of the main animal groups with a backbone. They are air-breathing with scaly bodies and, unlike amphibians, lay shelled eggs on land.

SAURISCHIAN
These were one of the two main types of dinosaurs and were 'lizard-hipped'. This group included the giant herbivororous sauropods as well as the theropod carnivores.

SAUROPODS
A group of huge herbivores that lived in herds. Diplodocus and Brachiosaurus *(right)* were sauropods.

SCAVENGER
A meat-eater that feeds on animals that are already dead, rather than prey it has killed.

SPECIES
A group of organisms that have a similar appearance and breed only among themselves.

THEROPODS
A group of lizard-hipped dinosaurs that were bipedal meat-eaters.

TRIASSIC
The first of the three periods in history that make up the Mesozoic era. Dinosaurs first appeared during this time, which lasted from around 250 to 205 mya.

VERTEBRAE
These small bones make up the spine of an animal.

YOUR DINOS!

WE KNOW YOU LIKE DINOSAURS AND WE'VE GOT THE PICTURES TO PROVE IT! TAKE A LOOK AT THESE FANTASTIC PICTURES FROM SOME OF WALKING WITH DINOSAURS' BIGGEST FANS.

EGGS-ELLENT JOKE!
What do you call a dino on stilts?
A highnosaur!

These two Iguanadon look well-matched, the question is will they be mates or will they fight?! Thanks to Hereford's Georgia Henley, aged 10 (left), and William Youdale (right), also aged 10, of Cambridge.

Terrific 'Tarbosaurus'! Thanks to Natalie Robinson.

Matthew East, aged 10, sent us this cool Triceratops that he drew.

Cool border! Thanks to Rhiannon Lewis, aged 9, for your fab Spinosaurus.

EGGS-ELLENT JOKE!
How did dinosaurs pass their exams?
With extinction!

EGGS-ELLENT JOKE!
What do you call a blind dinosaur?
Do-you-think Hesaurus?!

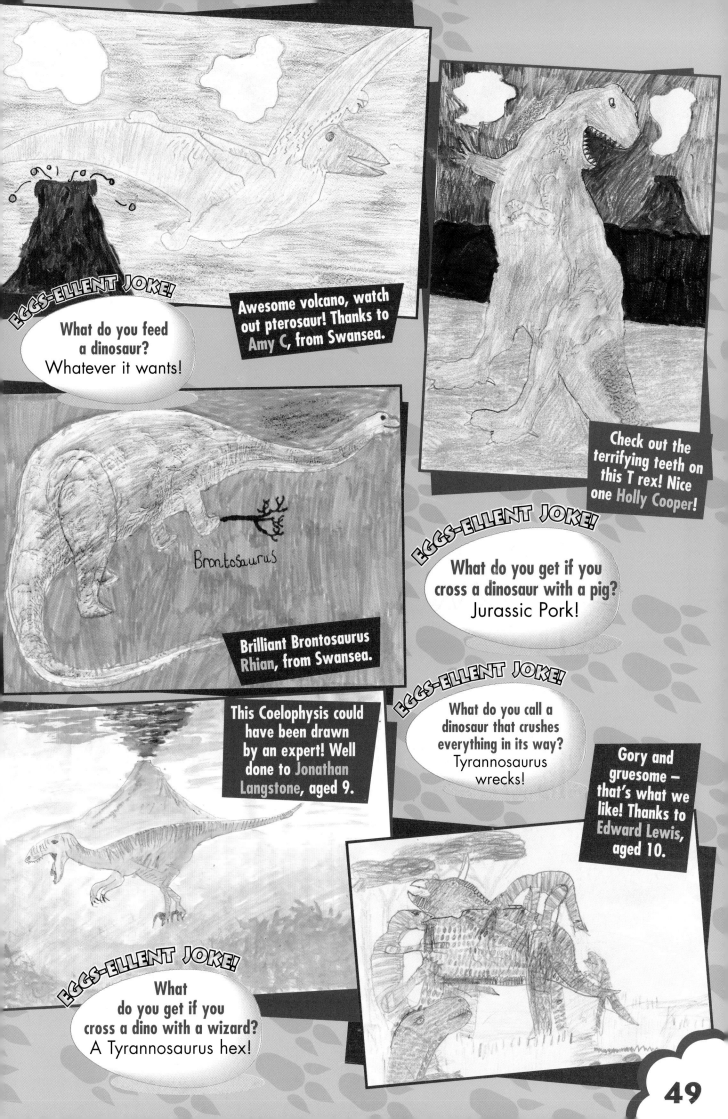

EGGS-ELLENT JOKE!

What do you feed a dinosaur?
Whatever it wants!

Awesome volcano, watch out pterosaur! Thanks to Amy C, from Swansea.

Check out the terrifying teeth on this T rex! Nice one Holly Cooper!

Brontosaurus

Brilliant Brontosaurus Rhian, from Swansea.

EGGS-ELLENT JOKE!

What do you get if you cross a dinosaur with a pig?
Jurassic Pork!

EGGS-ELLENT JOKE!

What do you call a dinosaur that crushes everything in its way?
Tyrannosaurus wrecks!

This Coelophysis could have been drawn by an expert! Well done to Jonathan Langstone, aged 9.

Gory and gruesome – that's what we like! Thanks to Edward Lewis, aged 10.

EGGS-ELLENT JOKE!

What do you get if you cross a dino with a wizard?
A Tyrannosaurus hex!

ART-O-SAURUS! 2

DUELLI DINOS!

GET THE DINO LOWDOWN ON HOW TO DRAW THESE MIGHTY DINOSAURS IN THE ULTIMATE BATTLE! THIS IS A TRICKY ONE, BUT GIVE IT A GO – UNLESS YOU'RE SCARED!

STEP ONE: Start by lightly sketching the main circle shapes for the bodies of both dinosaurs – Allosaurus' body circle should be more like a D. Then add the rough leg, arm and tail shapes like the ones in the picture.

STEP TWO: Fill in some details, like semi-circles on Ankylosaurus' back and small circles on his tail. Allosaurus has got tiger-like stripes instead. When it comes to their faces, draw the letter 'C', but backwards for Allosaurus! Then add what no meat-eating dino would be seen without – teeth and claws!

Rub out the circles and add some more details like we have here. Put some movement in their limbs – a few straight lines for wrinkles will do the job.

STEP THREE:

Don't panic if you can't draw this very well, they didn't live at the same time, so they would never have actually fought anyway!

STEP FOUR: Add some colour and your finishing touches. Now you're ready to roar!

MODEL

BEHIND THE SCENES

WALKING WITH DINOSAURS

WHILE THE FILM CREWS WERE OUT ON LOCATION, THERE WAS A TEAM OF PEOPLE LEFT AT HOME. THEIR TASK WAS TO TAKE THE ACCURATE DINOSAUR MODELS MADE EARLIER AND TO BRING THEM TO LIFE...

Back at London's Framestore, Mike Milne and his team set to work.

1 Scanning and Modelling

The first task was to get the highly-accurate dinosaur models into the computer so that they could be made to move again. This was done by scanning the models in a special machine that used laser beams to make a three-dimensional model of each dinosaur inside the computer.

2 Skin Design

The next step was to put some colour in their cheeks! Palaeontologists were called to the rescue again! But there simply isn't any fossilised skin to base any colour decisions on. So the most sensible solution was to look at animals in the wild today. Do they come in bright pink spots or do they blend in? Are they patterned with stripes, do they have brightly coloured crests for display? Although we couldn't be sure about dinosaur colours, Walking with Dinosaurs is thought to be the best guess based on what we currently know.

3 Animation

It was now possible to make their limbs and joints move again. But nobody had ever seen a dinosaur move in real life, so how did Walking with Dinosaurs get the dinosaurs to walk?

Yet again it was the scientists who saved the day. They looked at the way in which dinosaur bones fit together and then compared this to the way that modern animals move. It was thus possible to get

Coelophysis is brought to life by animators:
1. Basic scan **2.** Skeleton added to guide movement **3.** Action model without detail **4.** Final model with skin design added.

MAGIC!

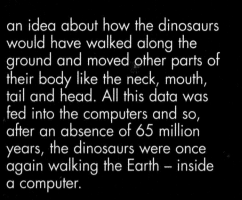

an idea about how the dinosaurs would have walked along the ground and moved other parts of their body like the neck, mouth, tail and head. All this data was fed into the computers and so, after an absence of 65 million years, the dinosaurs were once again walking the Earth – inside a computer.

4 Lighting and Rendering

Two years after starting the project, all that was needed was to put the computerised dinosaurs on to the film background – not an easy task!

One of the breakthroughs achieved by Walking with Dinosaurs was the realistic way in which the animals seemed to react with their environment. Instead of just looking like cartoon animals, these dinosaurs had to have shadows, leave footprints, eat plants (and each other!) as well as walk, run, swim and fly. To achieve this took months of hard work by a large team of people.

Every second of film had to be carefully put together. First of all the dinosaurs in the computers were combined with the film that had been shot abroad. Just placing the dinosaurs on to the film was not good enough. To make them look really realistic special computers were used to add in the small details that were filmed separately, like making sure that the dinosaurs had shadows and made clouds of dust when they ran.

Lastly, the dinosaurs had to be given voices. Again, nobody has

ever heard a dinosaur roar, but the size of their mouths, throats and noses does give us a clue as to the sort of noises they would have made. So do the noises of large living reptiles like crocodiles and the Komodo dragon. Once the dinosaurs had been given their voices the series was complete and ready to be seen on television.

Thanks to Walking with Dinosaurs it has been possible to see how the dinosaurs might have actually lived when they were alive. It had taken three years to make, but the end result was worth it!

While on location, bushes, plants, rock, trees and driftwood were filmed against bluescreen backgrounds and dust clouds and splashes were similarly filmed in the studio. This would help make the dinosaurs look as though they were really there, interacting with their environments.

HOW TO BRING A DINOSAUR TO LIFE!

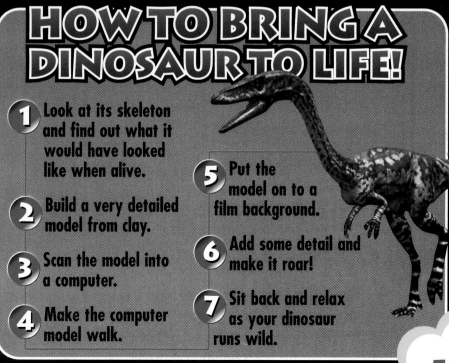

1. Look at its skeleton and find out what it would have looked like when alive.

2. Build a very detailed model from clay.

3. Scan the model into a computer.

4. Make the computer model walk.

5. Put the model on to a film background.

6. Add some detail and make it roar!

7. Sit back and relax as your dinosaur runs wild.

DINOSAUR

GREAT, GREAT, GREAT AUNTY
DIPLODOCUS ("DIPPY")
AGED 150 MYA

● **DIPLODOCUS**

Length: 30m.
Height: 5m at hip.
Weight: 20 tonnes.
Group: Sauropods.
Lived: Late Jurassic, 155-145 mya.
Eating habits: Herbivore, so ate leaves and soft plants like ferns.
Walked: On four legs – quadruped.
Distinctive features: Check out that enormous whip-like tail! Some say it might have been used for communication.
Fantastic facts: Diplodocus was the longest animal ever to have walked the earth, but its brain was only the size of a fist.

FAMILY ALBUM

THE BABY OF THE FAMILY
TYRANNOSAURUS REX ("JUNIOR")
AGED 66 MYA

● **TYRANNOSAURUS REX**

Length: Up to 14m.
Height: About 6m at hip.
Weight: 5 tonnes.
Group: Theropods.
Lived: Late Cretaceous, 67-65 mya.
Eating habits: Meat-eater – carnivore.
Walked: On two legs – biped.
Distinctive features: Big-headed bully! The T rex had a very big head which looked odd sat on his short neck, especially with his tiny arms as well.
Fantastic facts: This meat-eater had quite a mouthful! When open, his mouth was a metre wide and with just one bite he could tear off up to 70kg meat. He could swallow you whole!

Watch out – Junior's on the prowl!

COLOSSAL CROSSWORD

1 p l a n t s **2** s · · **3** · **4** · **5** f · · · · **6** t e e t h **7** h
· **A** · · **8** c · · · · · · · · f · **9** e · · · · · · · · · · e
· · · · a · · · · · · · o · u · · · · · · · · · · r
· · · · l · · **10** · · · s · s · · · · · · · · · b
11 · · · · e s · · **12** · · · i · t · · **13** · · · · v
· · · · · · · · · · · l · r · · · · · · · o
16 · · **17** · · **18** · · · · s e · · · · · · **15** · r
· · · · · · · **19** · **20** · · · p · · · **21** r e
· · · · · · · · · · · t · · · · u s
24 · · · **25** **26** · · · · o · · · · **27** r · b
C · · · · · · **28** **29** · n · · · · · · · ·
· · · · · · · **30** h o t · · · · ·
· · · · **31** · **32** · y · · · · · · · ·
33 · · · · · l · · · · · · ·
· · · · · u · · · · · · ·
· · · **34** · · · s · · · · · · ·
35 · · · · · · · · · · · · · ·

ANSWERS

ACROSS: 1) plants; 6) teeth; 8) carnivores; 10) claws; 11) swim; 12) dad; 14) species; 16) cannibal; 19) egg; 21) rare;
22) allosaur; 24) skin; 25) dino; 27) be; 28) wing; 30) hot; 31) jaw; 33) ice; 34) reptile; 35) omnivores.
DOWN: 1) postosuchus; 2) scales; 3) crocodile; 4) lizards; 5) fossils; 7) herbivores; 9) eustreptospondylus; 13) fin; 15)
share; 17) noon; 18) bird; 20) grow; 21) rub; 23) leg; 26) insect; 29) injure; 32) winter.

1. Herbivores eat these! (6 letters)

6. Don't get too close, they might take a bite out of you if they're attached to a dino's jaw! (5)

8. These guys were meat-eaters who dined on different dinos! (10)

10. Dinos didn't have fingernails, they had sharp _ _ _ _ _ instead! (5)

11. Liopleurodons do this, and hopefully you would too if you lived in the sea! (4)

12. Dinosaur mums were protective of their children, but you wouldn't want to mess with a baby dino's _ _ _ either! (3)

14. The scientific name for one of the same animal type or specimen. (7)

16. Some dinos weren't picky about who they ate – even one of their own kind. (8)

19. Which came first, the chicken? Baby dinosaurs would disagree! (3)

21. Re-arrange R E A R, to find this uncommon word. (4)

22. See **picture A**, for this dinosaur group. (8)

24. Another word for flesh? It covers your body and dinosaurs had it too. (4)

25. My name is dinosaur but you can call me this for short! (4)

27. _ _ ware of the dinosaur! (2)

28. The arm of a bird is called this. (4)

30. Some dinos lived in cold regions, others liked their weather to be _ _ _. (3)

31. See **picture B**. The meat-eater's was powerful and held sharp, spiky teeth. (3)

33. When it is so cold that everything freezes, _ _ _ forms. (3)

34. Dinosaurs, crocodiles, snakes and lizards all belong to this animal family. (7)

35. Humans are these because our bodies are adapted to eat both meat and veg! (9)

DOWN

1. See **picture C** to find out the name of this carnivorous reptile. (11)

2. A reptile's skin is usually covered in these. They can weigh you too! (6)

3. See you later, alligator! This fishy snapper didn't die out with the dinosaurs. (9)

4. Unscramble the letters to find the name of these reptiles: R D Z S I L A. (7)

5. Palaeontologists study these rocks to find out about ancient life. (7)

7. Animals which only eat plants fit into this category – if they were human, they'd be called vegetarians! (10)

9. See **picture D** for this meaty snacker! (18)

13. The fish needs this to help him swim – he'd be finished without it! (3)

15. To give up some food and offer it to another. Unlikely act for most dino diners! (5)

17. Another word for 12pm. (4)

18. Wings, beak, feathers – get the picture? (4)

20. To get bigger and develop. (4)

21. The missing letters, but backwards: MUTTA _ _ _ RASAURUS. (3)

23. Some walked on two _ _ _ s, other dinosaurs were quadropeds. (3)

26. This creature will bug you, it's a bit of a pest! (6)

29. Claws, teeth and swiping tails can _ _ _ _ _ _ _ you. (7)

32. The coldest of the four seasons! (6)

DINO DEATH

WAS IT A VOLCANO? WAS IT ALIENS? DID THEY RUN OUT OF FOOD? DINOS ARE DEAD BUT WE DON'T KNOW WHY – CHECK OUT WHAT THE KNOW-ALLS SAY !

THE FACTS:

1 The last known dinosaur fossils are found in rocks that are 65 million years old.

2 After this time the dinosaurs are completely absent from the fossil records.

3 This sudden disappearance of the dinosaurs has been a mystery that has perplexed scientists for over 150 years.

4 Many different reasons for the dinosaurs' extinction have been put forward but we still don't know the reason today!

Here are some of the more popular (and weirder!) theories...

Asteroid of Doom!

In 1980, the father and son team of Walter and Luis Alvarez suggested that a giant asteroid from space, about the size of Bermuda, may have smashed into the Earth, killing the dinosaurs and many other types of plant and animals. They had found a large amount of a rare element called iridium in a rock layer very close to the last known dinosaur fossils. Iridium is also found inside asteroids and the Alvarezes thought that the iridium could have come from a large asteroid. An asteroid hitting the Earth would have had a terrible effect on the world's environment, throwing up millions of tons of ash and dust into the air, blocking out the sun for months, or even years, and causing the Earth's surface to freeze. The dinosaurs were the largest and most specialised animals on Earth and probably couldn't survive such low temperatures. Other scientists say the asteroid could also have started forest fires and may have even poisoned the oceans, killing much marine life. As much as half of all the life on Earth may have been killed in only a few months.

In 1990, a team of scientists in Mexico discovered what could be the crater. Unfortunately, it's buried under 2km of rock and so is difficult to study, but this and the iridium are evidence that an asteroid may have hit the Earth at around the time the dinosaurs became extinct.

THE BIG MYSTERY!

Vicious Volcanoes

Shortly after the Alvarezes announced their asteroid theory, another group of scientists made an interesting discovery. They found evidence that around 65 mya there were volcanoes in India that gushed vast amounts of lava, which can still be seen today. These volcanoes were some of the largest ever found by geologists and were at their most active when the dinosaurs became extinct. Could this be just a coincidence? Some scientists think that these volcanoes may have put enough ash and poisonous gases into the air to damage the Earth's environment and cause the dinosaurs and other animals to become extinct over a period of several thousand years or longer. What's more, the volcanoes in India also produced the element iridium. It has been

suggested that these volcanoes could have been the source of the iridium that the Alvarezes found in 1980. The volcano theory is thought by many to be a strong alternative to the idea of an asteroid impact killing the dinosaurs.

A Gradual Decline

Before either the asteroid or volcano ideas were proposed, it was thought the dinosaurs became extinct because of natural changes in the world over millions of years. Recent discoveries have led some scientists to support this idea again. It is now thought that dinosaur numbers were declining for several million years before their last fossils are found. Also, some animals that were once thought to have become extinct 65 mya, such as the pterosaurs and much marine life, are now thought to have died out millions of years earlier than this. Scientists think that instead of an asteroid or volcanoes ending the reign of the dinosaurs, it could have been changes in the world's climate and oceans that killed the dinosaurs and other life on Earth. These climate changes would have taken place over millions of years and would have gradually killed the dinosaurs one by one until by 65 mya there were none left at all. Some people have compared the effects of this ancient climate change to today's problem of global warming which threatens many types of plant and animal on Earth today.

OUR SURVEY SAYS:

Nobody can say for sure what caused the dinosaurs to become extinct. An asteroid hitting the Earth has the most support but this does not explain all of what we know about the last days of the dinosaurs. Neither do gigantic volcanoes or changes in the world's climate. We do know that there were many things happening to the Earth in the few million years before the dinosaurs became extinct and that it was a time of great change for the plants and animals. Perhaps it was a combination of all of these events.

DINOS TODAY

There are many museums which have great displays of marine reptiles and dinosaurs.

There are also many clubs and societies that you can join. These can be great fun, but always ask what sort of level the talks and walks are aimed at... some talks even test the experts' ability to concentrate!

A good starting point for any budding bone-hunter is their local museum, or even ask a teacher who might know a geologist. You could also look up your local geological society through your school or museum. Get digging!

FOR MORE INFORMATION ABOUT ALL ASPECTS OF DINOSAURS, CONTACT: THE DINOSAUR SOCIETY, PO BOX 188, HITCHIN, HERTS, SG5 1GQ. TELEPHONE 01462 626686 www.dinosoc.org

BELFAST
National Museums and Galleries of Northern Ireland
01232 383000

BIRMINGHAM
Museum and Art Gallery
0121 303 2834

CAMBRIDGE
Sedgwick Museum
Department of Earth Sciences
University of Cambridge
01223 333456

CARDIFF
National Museum and Gallery
01222 397951

DORCHESTER
The Dinosaur Museum
01305 269880

EDINBURGH
National Museums of Scotland
0131 225 7534

GLASGOW
Hunterian Museum & Art Gallery
University of Glasgow
0141 330 4221

HORSHAM
Horsham Museum
01403 254959

ISLE OF WIGHT
Museum of Isle of Wight Geology
01983 404344

LEICESTER
New Walk Museum and Art Gallery
0116 255 4100

LONDON
Natural History Museum
0207 942 5000

LYME REGIS
Philpot Museum
01297 443370

MAIDSTONE
Maidstone Museum and Art Gallery
01622 754497

NORTH WALES
Dinosaur World
Eirias Park, Colwyn Bay
01492 518111
Check for opening times!

OXFORD
The University Museum
01865 272950

YORK
York Museum
01904 629745

Track down Walking with Dinosaurs on the web at:
www.bbc.co.uk/dinosaurs

MORE WEBSITES
www.nhm.ac.uk
www.dinodata.net
www.amnh.org/exhibitions
(American Museum of Natural History)
www.nmnh.si.edu/paleo/dino/dinohome
(Smithsonian Institution)